D1105182

STACKS

CHILDREN'S LIBRARY
5201 WOODWARD AVENUE
DETROIT, MICHIGAN 48202-4093
833-1490

CL

How Is a Pencil Made?

Angela Royston

Heinemann Library
Chicago, Illinois

© 2005 Heinemann Library
a division of Reed Elsevier Inc.
Chicago, Illinois

Customer Service   888–454–2279

Visit our website at www.heinemannlibrary.com

All rights reserved. No part of this publication may be reproduced or transmitted in any form or by any means, electronic or mechanical, including photocopying, recording, taping, or any information storage and retrieval system, without permission in writing from the publisher.

Photo research by Melissa Allison and
Debra Weatherley
Designed by Jo Hinton-Malivoire and AMR
Printed and bound in China by South China Printing Company

09 08 07 06 05
10 9 8 7 6 5 4 3 2 1

Library of Congress Cataloging-in-Publication Data
Royston, Angela.
  How is a pencil made? / Angela Royston.
      p. cm. -- (How are things made?) (Heinemann library)
Includes bibliographical references and index.
   ISBN 1-4034-6640-8 (hc. : library binding) -- ISBN 1-4034-6647-5
(pbk.)
1. Pencils--Juvenile literature. I. Title. II. Series. III. Series:
Heinemann first library
TS1268.R69 2005
674'.88--dc22

                              2004016526

Acknowledgments
The author and publisher are grateful to the following for permission to reproduce copyright material: Alamy Images p.**7**; Corbis pp.**22** (Bob Krist), **9** (Lester Lefkowitz), **13** (Tony Arruza)**;** Corbis Royalty Free pp. **26**, **28**; Digital Vision p. **4**; Getty Images/ ImageBank p.**12**; Getty Images/ Photodisc p.**28**; Harcourt Education Ltd pp.**21**, **29**; Harcourt Education Ltd/Tudor Photography p. **27**; Norman Chambers pp. **6**, **8**, **10**, **11**, **16**, **17**, **18**, **19**, **20**, **23**, **24**, **25**; Powerstock pp.**14/15** (Ken Welsh).

Cover photograph of pencils reproduced with permission of Harcourt Education Ltd/Tudor Photography.

Every effort has been made to contact copyright holders of any material reproduced in this book. Any omissions will be rectified in subsequent printings if notice is given to the publisher.

Some words are shown in bold, **like this.** You can find out what they mean by looking in the glossary.

Contents

What Is in a Pencil?

We use pencils for writing and drawing. This pencil has **lead** in it. The eraser on the end rubs out any mistakes.

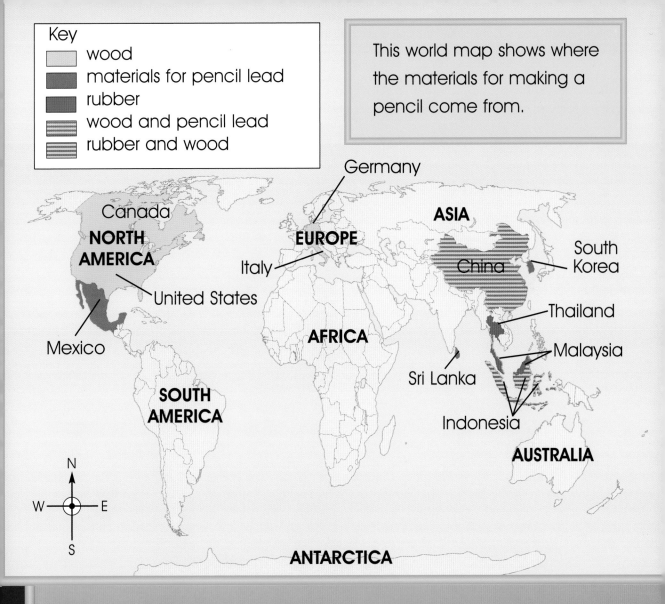

Key
- wood
- materials for pencil lead
- rubber
- wood and pencil lead
- rubber and wood

This world map shows where the materials for making a pencil come from.

Germany

Canada

NORTH AMERICA

EUROPE

ASIA

China

South Korea

Italy

United States

Thailand

Mexico

AFRICA

Malaysia

Sri Lanka

SOUTH AMERICA

Indonesia

AUSTRALIA

N
W — E
S

ANTARCTICA

A pencil is made of different **materials**. The main part is usually wood. The materials used to make pencils come from many different parts of the world.

5

Who Makes Pencils?

Several different **companies** have factories that make pencils. Many people work for each company.

Some people work the machines in the factory.

Several people work in offices. Some of the workers decide how many pencils to make. Other workers buy the **materials** to make the pencils.

Where the Wood Comes From

Wood from incense cedar trees is the best wood for making pencils. The trees are cut down and left for several months. This is called seasoning.

These trees are specially grown to be made into pencils.

The wood is cut into thin strips called slats.

The thin **slats** of wood are soaked in **wax** and **stain**. The slats are dried and then sent to the pencil factory.

The Pencil Lead

The part of the pencil that marks the paper is called the **lead**, but it is not actually lead. Instead it is a mixture of **clay**, **graphite**, and water. The mixture is called **blacklead**.

graphite

clay

Some of the water is squeezed out of the mixture. The blacklead mixture is pushed through machines. The machines shape the lead into a long, thin stick. The stick is cut into strips, then dried and baked in an oven.

Hard or Soft?

Some pencils have a hard **lead**. Others have a soft lead. There is more **graphite** in softer leads. Artists like to draw with the softest leads.

Stonemasons use the hardest leads to write on stone.

Most people write with HB pencils. These are hard (H) and black (B). There is more **clay** in harder leads.

Colored Pencils

Colored pencils are good for drawing and coloring. The **lead** in colored pencils is made of **clay**, **wax**, and colored **chemicals**.

The **materials** in colored lead are mixed together. Then they are squeezed out through a machine into a long, thin stick. The stick is not baked but left to dry in a special room.

Colored pencils are made in many different colors.

Adding the Pencil Lead

Each **slat** is as long as a single pencil. Each slat is as wide as nine pencils. A machine cuts nine narrow **grooves** side by side along the slat.

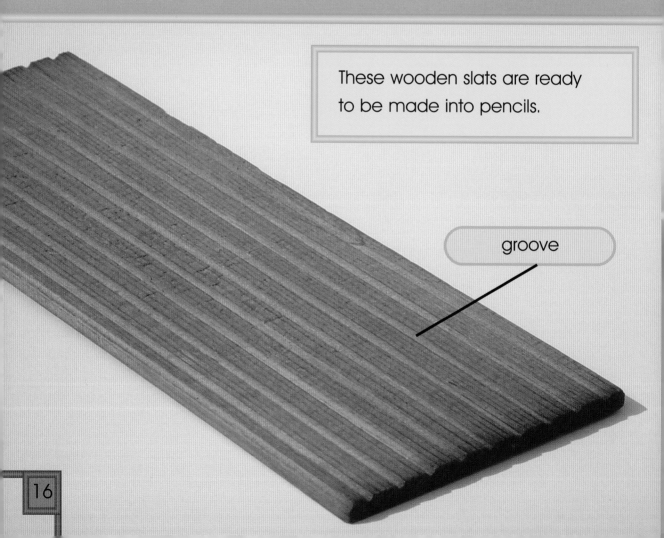

These wooden slats are ready to be made into pencils.

groove

The grooves are covered with glue.
Then a pencil **lead** is placed into each
groove. The lead is the same length as
the finished pencil.

A Pencil Sandwich

Grooves are cut into a second **slat**. Then this slat is placed over the first slat. The two slats are glued together to make a pencil sandwich.

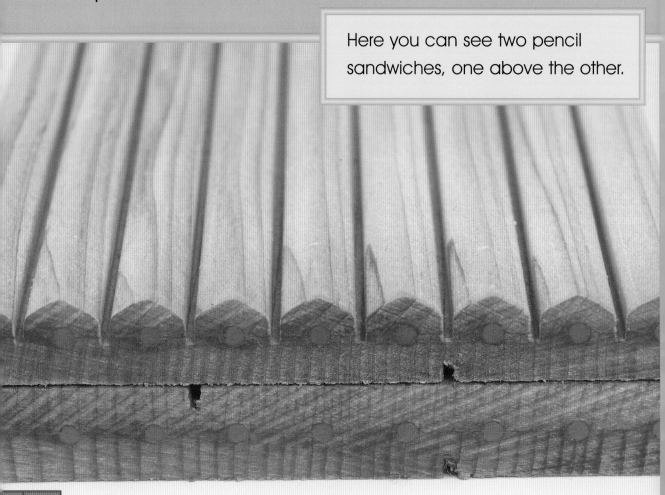

Here you can see two pencil sandwiches, one above the other.

A machine cuts the pencil sandwiches into separate pencils. Some pencils are round, but most have six flat sides.

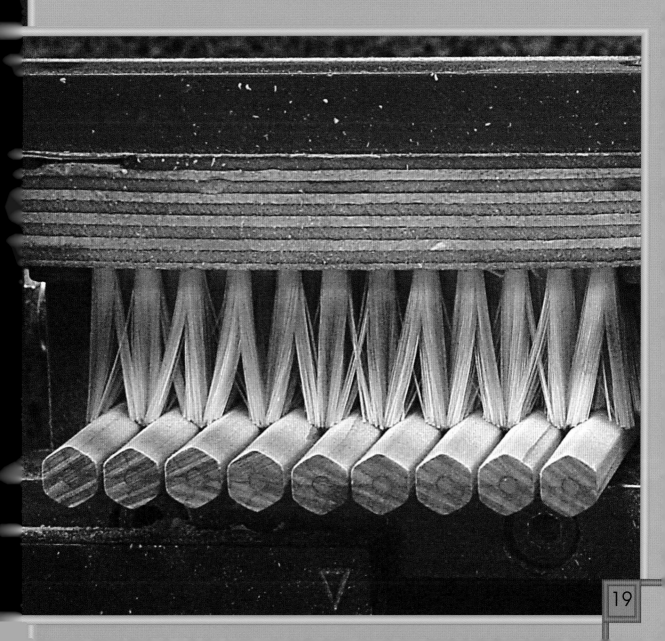

Finishing the Outside

The outside of the pencil is painted. Many pencils are painted yellow. The **company's** name is stamped onto the paint.

HB

The letters H and B are stamped on to show how hard and black the pencil is. In some countries the pencil is sharpened into a point.

The Eraser

Many pencils have an eraser on the end. The eraser is usually made of **synthetic rubber** or of plastic. Some erasers are made of real rubber.

Rubber is made from the thick white juice of rubber trees.

To attach the eraser to the pencil, metal bands are put onto the end of the pencil. **Conveyor** belts carry the pencils and the metal **bands** to the next stage.

metal band

Attaching the Eraser to the Pencil

A machine heats long strips of eraser. When the strips are cool, the machine cuts them into many small pieces.

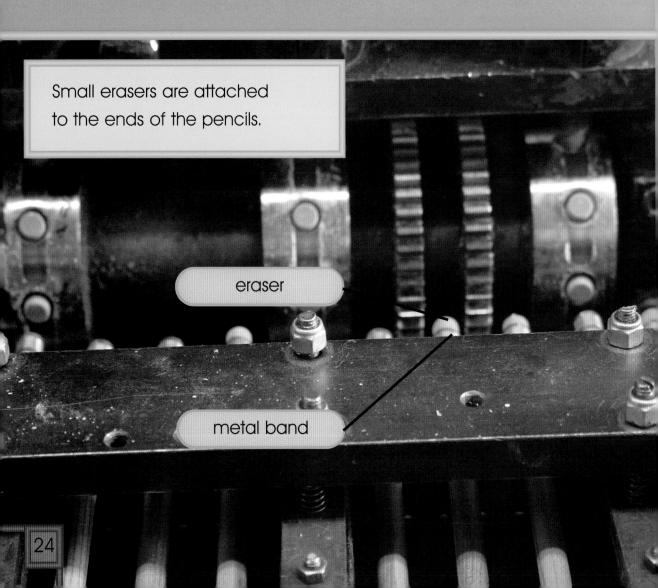

Small erasers are attached to the ends of the pencils.

eraser

metal band

The machine tightens the metal
band around the eraser and the
end of each pencil.

Selling the Pencils

The pencils are put into boxes. A truck takes them to a **warehouse**. They are stored in the warehouse until a store orders some pencils.

The store sells the pencils. Some of the money you pay goes to the pencil **company**. The pencil company uses some of the money to make more pencils.

From Start to Finish

A pencil is made mainly from the wood of an incense cedar tree. The wood is cut into **slats**. **Grooves** are cut into the slats.

Leads made from **clay** and **graphite** are dropped into the grooves.

A pencil sandwich is cut into separate pencils.

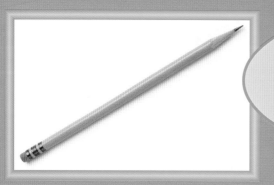

An eraser is attached to the end of the pencil with a metal **band**.

A Closer Look

The print on the side of a pencil gives the pencil **company**'s name and the kind of lead in the pencil.

type of lead

Glossary

band thin strip that is made into a loop

blacklead mixture of graphite, clay, and water

chemical substance that things are made of

clay kind of mud. Clay is mainly used for making pottery.

company group of people who work together

conveyor belt machine that carries things on a long loop from one place to another

graphite soft material used to make pencil leads

groove long narrow rut

lead part of a pencil that makes a mark on paper

materials what things are made of

slat thin strip of wood

stain liquid used to color wood and keep it from rotting

synthetic material material made from plastic or coal

warehouse building where things are stored

wax material that candles are made from

More Books to Read

Geller, Kristin. *Follow the Directions and Draw It All by Yourself!* New York: Instructor, 2001.

Gibson, Ray, and Amanda Barlow and Fiona Watt. *I Can Draw People*. Toledo: Usborne, 2002.

Gibson, Ray, and Amanda Barlow and Felicity Everett. *What Shall I Draw?* Toledo: Usborne, 2002.

Index